Social Networking in Recruitment

Build your social networking expertise to give yourself
a cost-effective advantage in the hiring market

Amanda Belton

Impackt Publishing

We Mean Business

Social Networking in Recruitment

First published: February 2014

Production Reference: 1250214

Published by Impackt Publishing Ltd.
Livery Place
35 Livery Street
Birmingham B3 2PB, UK.

ISBN 978-1-78300-004-3

www.Impacktpub.com

Cover Image by Jarek Blaminsky (milak6@wp.pl)

Credits

Author
Amanda Belton

Project Coordinator
Priyanka Goel

Proofreaders
Maria Gould
Paul Hindle

Copy Editors
Jalasha D'costa
Maria Gould
Paul Hindle

Production Coordinator
Melwyn D'sa

Cover Work
Melwyn D'sa

Reviewers
Manavendra S.Gokhale
Marianne Steen

Commissioning Editor
Nick Falkowski

About the Author

Amanda Belton is an IT manager specializing in agile and lean software development. Over the past 20 years, she has worked in small startup companies and large multinational organizations with responsibility for recruiting the people who become productive and happy members of her team. This experience working with in-house recruitment specialists as well as agencies has led her to explore the ways social media supports recruitment efforts to find and engage with the right people in a tight labor market. She is a self-admitted geek who has learned from her mistakes and is willing to share the wisdom that she's learned the hard way.

About the Reviewers

Manavendra S.Gokhale is a management professional with 24 years of experience, 17 years of which at CEO level. He has headed companies across multiple verticals, and has strong leadership and team-building capabilities. He has worked on MIS systems and analytics, and has evaluated people at various levels in numerous companies.

He is a visiting faculty member at various well-known business schools, where he teaches various subjects, including general management. He has experience working as a Corporate Consultant for eight years and has also conducted corporate workshops.

He has used IT extensively in his corporate activities and developed strong networking skills as a result of working across various verticals and engagements in India and abroad.

Manavendra defines progress as making things easier by encouraging people to reach their milestones by helping them avoid the problems they face and helping them learn by sharing experiences.

Marianne Steen is a Danish Internet pioneer and author of three Danish books on Internet job searching. As a consultant, she has provided web strategies and solutions for people looking for jobs and career development, as well as for companies looking for the best talent. From 2009 to 2013, she was a board member at two online recruitment companies. From 1997 to 2002, she was a director at MatchWork WorldWide. She also participated in launching the SAAS service in the UK, Sweden, and Germany. She has a Master's degree in Horticulture.

Some more on her company, Marianne Steen & Co. helps companies sourcing potential employees via social media and professionals to manage their professional digital profile and identity. Prodii.com, developed by Marianne Steen & Co., is a brand new service for companies that enables them to build dynamic company career pages, and is also meant for professionals to manage their professional data and digital footprint.

Contents

> Preface

Over the years, I've spent endless hours reading through CVs, trawling through candidate profiles, and conducting interviews. Sometimes I've done a good job of recruitment, and I have hired people who have excelled at and enjoyed their role, but sometimes I've failed and I have hired people who didn't stay because they and the role weren't the right fit. Right now, it's an exciting time to undertake recruitment as social networks provide highly effective ways to build relationships with potential candidates, and these relationship building activities mean as an employer, you get to know the candidates better over a period of time, and as a potential employee, you get an insight into whether the company and the role will be a good fit.

This book will build on your current knowledge and experience of recruitment to successfully integrate social media into your recruitment strategy to get the best possible results with a sustainable investment of time. It will take you through clear, practical steps to building a tailored approach that makes the most of the resources already available within your organization.

What this book covers

Chapter 1, Becoming a Digital Native, is a step-by-step approach to navigating social networks to find the people and communities with the skills and experience you're looking for in prospective employees.

Chapter 2, Forewarned is Forearmed – Being Prepared For a Crisis, considers the common risks of using social networks for recruitment while guiding you through a process to help you identify the unique risks for your organization.

Chapter 3, Pulling it All Together in a Plan, uses a learning approach to help you develop and adapt a strategic approach to using social networks for recruitment.

Who this book is for

This book is designed for HR and hiring managers who have a recruitment strategy in place and who want to reach prospective employees where they're already engaged and interacting with others. As a hiring organization, it's assumed you have already established your employer brand but are looking to expand this into the online world. As an individual, you are expected to have experience and knowledge of recruitment that you will then apply to social networks as a new channel for communicating and engaging with others.

Conventions

In this book, you will find a number of styles of text that distinguish between different kinds of information. Here are some examples of these styles, and an explanation of their meaning.

New terms and **important words** are shown in bold.

Make a note

Warnings or important notes appear in a box like this.

Tip

Tips and tricks appear like this.

Reader feedback

Feedback from our readers is always welcome. Let us know what you think about this book—what you liked or may have disliked. Reader feedback is important for us to develop titles that you really get the most out of.

To send us general feedback, simply send an e-mail to `contact@impacktpub.com`, and mention the book title via the subject of your message.

If there is a book that you need and would like to see us publish, please send us a note via the **Submit Idea** form on `https://www.impacktpub.com/#!/bookidea`.

Piracy

Piracy of copyright material on the Internet is an ongoing problem across all media. At Impackt, we take the protection of our copyright and licenses very seriously. If you come across any illegal copies of our works, in any form, on the Internet, please provide us with the location address or website name immediately so that we can pursue a remedy.

Please contact us at `copyright@impacktpub.com` with a link to the suspected pirated material.

We appreciate your help in protecting our authors, and our ability to bring you valuable content.

>1

Becoming a Digital Native

At its heart, recruitment is all about communication between organizations and people, that is, a process of communication and relationship building that leads to an eventual hire. How we communicate has changed dramatically over the past two decades; we can now reach a wide audience of professional and personal connections with an immediacy that would have been mind-boggling 20 years ago! These dramatic shifts have had a big impact on business roles that need to communicate with the wider public.

The "dinosaur" recruiters advertising on job boards online may not see the comet coming to drive them to extinction, but it's certainly on its way. There are whole groups of potential high-performing, highly-skilled employees hanging out with their friends and peers on different social networks. If you're looking to recruit a graduate, it's quite likely that if you're successful in reaching just a few in this demographic, then these few will also be connected to quite a large network of other graduates, all in the same city or town.

Similarly, if you're looking to recruit a senior IT professional, it's quite likely that if you're successful in tapping into one senior IT worker's network, then you've reached a larger group of people with similar experience and in your target location. That's not to say that job boards have no purpose, but you're reaching a relatively small audience of people actively searching these boards for their next job. Let's leave the dinosaurs to congregate in the one spot while we explore other, more hospitable environments for survival as a recruiter.

You are no doubt responsible for recruiting for many different types of roles, and reaching the right candidates means using the most appropriate platform: that may be through **Facebook** for graduates, **LinkedIn** for mid-career professionals, **Meetup** for professional specialties in short supply, or **Yammer** for internal candidates.

If your company has an online presence and employees who are active on social media, then you have an easy result...or do you?

For many senior managers, it's not good enough to delegate to those employees with the skills to engage successfully through social media: communication and relationship building for recruitment needs to be completely aligned to HR's recruitment strategy in order to achieve the business goals. Otherwise, we're all just sitting around laughing at grumpy cats together.

In this chapter, you're going to navigate your way through social networking platforms to find and connect with different communities. Once you've mastered the art of finding communities across multiple platforms as an individual, it will be simple to translate this to an organizational strategy to find and connect with your potential hires in their own communities.

Finding a mentor close to home

Have you noticed the ease with which some people take to the digital world? They're the ones tweeting on the bus to work, communicating with friends and colleagues through social networks and finding an intrinsic value in their time spent online. These **social mavens** may be using Yammer internally within an organization to engage in conversations that drive their work forward; they might be using Twitter to share and find links to useful work-related articles; they may volunteer as a community coordinator for a group's Facebook page; or they may successfully leverage LinkedIn's posts and conversation threads to engage with their professional network.

You may recognize a gap between your own capability as the HR or Recruiting Manager who needs to execute your hiring strategy and the social networking expertise of the social mavens in your organization. If this is the case, you can build the capability to connect a recruitment strategy with these online communication channels through a mentor.

Mentoring is an ideal way to build new skills, and the skills required for navigating social networks are best learned in a person-to-person way in this kind of trusted learning environment.

Using an internal social network

If your organization uses Yammer, it becomes quite easy to identify a potential mentor. You can use the Yammer leaderboard to identify people who are active on this enterprise microblogging platform, and once you've followed them, you can start to pick out who are the good role models you'd like to learn from. They may even refer to their activity on external social networking platforms such as their blogs or their Twitter feed. This helps identify those social mavens with the skills and experience you can learn from.

Tip

Type the name (or Twitter handle if you know it) of a few of your likely mentors into a free tool such as `Klout.com` and gauge their influence.

Using an external professional network

Another approach is to connect with your company's LinkedIn groups. If you haven't already, now is a good time to set up your LinkedIn profile. When you log in, you'll find that the platform is quite good at suggesting "groups you may like", which will include fellow employees. Once you're connected to fellow employees, you'll notice your feed showing posts by colleagues actively participating in discussions. It becomes easy to identify who is an active and positive participant in valuable discussions on this professional networking platform.

Using an external social network

Yet another good way to find your mentor is to approach your graduate program employees to find whether they have a Facebook or LinkedIn group that they use to connect with each other. I expect you'll find they'll be pleased to have you join their community where you'll have the opportunity to interact with and observe the most active participants.

Your selected mentor will hopefully provide you with excellent learning opportunities as you build your confidence in navigating social networks. Later in the book, we'll be using these same strategies to identify influencers and active community members to drive your recruitment strategy.

Finding your voice on Twitter

Imagine how difficult it would be for someone to learn how to swim from an instruction manual: can you picture the poor sap jumping into the pool, only to find that those first few seconds underwater where they feel like they're drowning aren't adequately covered in the how-to guide. When you first start seeing the volume of information flowing from an information-sharing platform such as Twitter, it can feel a lot like drowning. We'll now take some time to build your expertise in making sense of the information deluge that you'll get from Twitter. Your expertise will then be put to good use in working out how to reach your potential candidates who likewise are paddling in a river of information of Amazonian proportions.

Let's work out what kind of commitment you can make: can you devote 10 minutes of your daily morning commute over a two month period? Or, will it be easier to find 10 minutes on the iPad at the end of each work day?

However you can find this time, there's great benefit in setting aside regular small chunks of time to find your way on Twitter's microblogging platform. Along the way, we'll build a better understanding of the principles behind social networks and start to form a view of the approaches that will translate from a personal strategy to an organizational approach.

We're going to take a staged approach to build your level of comfort and limit your exposure to the wider online world until you're ready. The stages we'll go through are to firstly listen to a few people, then to speak out to the **Twitterverse**, and finally to engage in a conversation with a wider group of people on Twitter:

> ➤ **Day 1**: Set up your Twitter account at `twitter.com`. Remember that your bio is your business card. In 160 characters, you need to establish your identity as a real person (not a *spambot*) and provide a guide to your interests. Don't forget the photo!

> ➤ **Weeks 1 – 2**: Discover interesting people to follow—this is the fun bit! Follow recruitment thought leaders, politicians, comedians, and colleagues; basically anyone you might find interesting. This will set you up to understand how to make sense of the huge volume of information across multiple subjects that will flow to you through Twitter.

Make a note

Using Twitter apps such as **TweetDeck** or **HootSuite** will make Twitter much easier to navigate. You can categorize information into meaningful groups; for example, I like to see a stream of information for professional interests, a stream for colleagues, and another stream for local news.

➤ **Weeks 3 – 4**: Retweet an interesting and useful post each day. Do this consistently and with good judgment, and at this stage, you may find you're starting to gather followers. Continue to find new people to follow.

➤ **Weeks 5 – 6**: Build **lists** to structure the information flowing into your Twitter feed, and use **hashtags** to find more interesting information. Continue to retweet each day.

➤ **Weeks 7 – 8**: Reply to a tweet that catches your eye; you might answer a question that's been posed or add your comment to a statement. Tweet a link to an article you've found outside of Twitter, which may be an online newspaper or professional article. Continue to retweet each day.

➤ **Week 9 and beyond**: Aim to find a balance of retweets and original tweets. Start to engage with other Twitter users through replies to other tweets.

You should find you're now following a variety of topics and finding ways to make sense of the flow of information. Over time, you'll have built a flow of information that's valuable to you through following new people, unfollowing hashtags that aren't useful any longer, and connecting to groups of people online.

Finding your own community online

Now that you're on your way to mastering the Twitterverse, let's take a look at how communities come together on social networking sites. Once you've found your own way to find the communities you'd like to be part of, you'll have developed an understanding of what holds diverse communities together; you'll then be able to apply this to build a community around your organization's brand.

So, let's find your communities, those groups of like-minded individuals you'd like to connect with in your personal and professional life. Are you a new mum? A commuter cycling to work each day? A football fan? A photography enthusiast? Whatever you're in to, there's a community online to feed your personal and professional interests. As we'll discover, the ways that you find and connect with your community are the ways your recruitment strategy will seek to engage with potential employees.

Here are some ways to find your community:

➤ **Twitter hashtags**: Hashtags are a way people categorize their Twitter posts, linking it to other posts in the same category. For example, the hash tag *#careeradvice* is used by many recruiters with followers who are actively looking for work. If you see a few posts from an interesting Twitter user, you can navigate their network to see who they follow to find some more interesting people.

> ➤ **Meetup.com:** Strangely enough, this online platform is an ideal way to connect in real life with like-minded individuals in a specific geographic area. For example, I'm passionate about software development practices, so I've searched for this along with my home town and I've connected with a great group of people with a shared interest.

> ➤ **Blogs:** Some people are amazingly generous with their time providing regular, thoughtful web blog entries; the challenge is to find these people's blogs among the chaff of inane and badly written blogs that are out there. For example, if you're a keen cyclist doing a regular commute and you do an Internet search for "blogs", "cycling", and "commute", you'll find some blogs of varying quality. Once you've found a blog you like, you may find they reference other good quality blogs.

> ➤ **Yammer groups:** If your organization uses Yammer, you have a ready-made community with your colleagues. For example, you may find that a Yammer group already exists for fellow football fans, or you may need to start a group where people discuss the sport and their favorite teams.

You may notice we've been using a search to find someone interesting, then navigating through their publicly-known social network to find more people with a similar interest. This means we're quickly finding people who are worth listening to rather than just searching online against keywords. The people we find interesting are more likely to connect with other people we'd also be interested in.

This principle applies to recruiting for different roles, since most of your target employees aren't following your company's digital presence, and they may not even be actively looking for a job. Finding and connecting to your target candidates, who may not be actively looking for work, becomes a matter of finding and connecting to the right communities.

Summary

As you can see, there are a lot of new environments to play in if you're involved in recruitment right now. In this chapter, you've looked at how to find the social mavens in your organization and how to identify a suitable mentor. You've taken the first steps to finding your voice on Twitter and you've navigated different social networking platforms to connect to some very different communities online. Hopefully, your mentoring relationship is supporting you through your efforts to become a digital native.

Later in the book, you'll build on the understanding and strategies you've applied here to find your own community to do the same to find your target employees. You'll also look at how to build your own community around an employer brand that encourages and builds a strong relationship between a potential candidate and the organization. If you can build an online relationship with your target candidates, it's much the same as other social situations; they'll be much more receptive to your recruitment message if you already have a relationship together.

2

Forewarned is Forearmed – Being Prepared for a Crisis

We all remember that feeling as a kid when you had to leap across the room and into bed to avoid the monsters lurking in the dark corners, just out of sight. Some organizations have acted the same way, allowing a fear of the unknown risks and issues of this relatively new medium prevent them from realizing the benefits of these powerful channels for connecting with the right people. Social networks are an ideal channel for communication and building relationships that can lead to the employment of productive and engaged employees. Now, let's drag those monsters out from under the bed, give them names, and work out how to contain them!

In this chapter we'll identify the general and unique risks and challenges that face recruitment through social networking in your particular industry. We'll then consider updating or generating a social media policy and ready responses to arm you and your team with the appropriate tools to manage these potential issues.

Identifying risks and challenges

Recruitment is a high-stakes game: hire the wrong person and you do untold damage to your team's performance, act unfairly during the process and you will be breaking laws, lose a candidate at the last stage and you may be introducing costly delays as well as writing off the time and energy that has been invested in the hiring process.

We know the general risks of recruitment, whether the process be conducted through job boards or through more modern means. There are also general risks inherent in using social networks as a means of communication and engaging with people outside your company: reputational risks, legal and legislative risks, confidentiality and privacy risks, all of which apply to the recruitment process. Then, there are the unique risks that depend on the type of business: for example, a finance business operating under their country's prudential oversight would face different risks to a health research organization with competitive and ethical concerns around communication through social media.

What are the risks for your organization when you conduct recruitment activities through social networks? Let's step through a process to create a list of the risks that apply to your recruitment activities:

> ➤ Identify who can help identify risks for recruitment activities: this may include representatives from your legal team, marketing, HR, recruiting managers, and employees with a strong social media presence

> ➤ Establish your focusing question to guide an exploration of risks and challenges: this may be as simple as "We're opening up public conversations about working for ACME Corporation on Facebook, Twitter, and LinkedIn, what could go wrong?"

> ➤ Undertake a workshop or brainstorming session to identify the risks and challenges with your key representatives with the following agenda items:

>> ➢ Brief recap of social recruiting strategy

>> ➢ Brainstorming using the focusing question

>> ➢ Group risks into categories, for example, reputational, legal, confidentiality, and so on

>> ➢ Assess likelihood and potential impact of risks

>> ➢ Determine next steps

A sample list of risks identified for a healthcare organization might look like this:

Risk	Category	Likelihood	Potential impact
Candidates' discussion on a Facebook page inadvertently reveals confidential commercial information	Commercial confidence	Low	High
LinkedIn profile or post reveals results of recruitment process before all candidates are notified	Privacy	Medium	Medium
Someone registers a false careers page for the organization	Reputational	Medium	High

Risk	Category	Likelihood	Potential impact
Employee blog linked to from careers page includes opinions not endorsed by the organization or criticism of some practices	Reputational	Low	Medium
Current patient replies to Twitter posts with complaints about their treatment	Reputational	High	Medium
Candidate complains about fairness of recruitment process on a Facebook page	Reputational and legal	Low	High

Social media policy

Unlike those monsters under children's beds, there are very real and very frightening issues for employees and organizations interacting through social media. Let's line up some of the ugly and scary issues that have arisen in recent times:

> ➤ Companies have been sued for wrongful dismissal after firing workers making disparaging comments online about their employers

> ➤ Employees have inadvertently disclosed confidential commercial information to the whole world through actions on social networking sites

> ➤ Employees have disclosed private information about their clients to their Facebook connections

> ➤ Company Facebook pages have had supplier complaints posted that have spread through the social network to thousands of people before being picked up by media outlets

I encourage you to take a fresh look at your company's social media policy: does it clearly specify the rules and guidelines for your staff, does it align with your company values, is it brief and written in simple language that is memorable and easily understood, and does it describe the consequences for policy violation?

There are some fantastic examples of social media policies freely available online with valuable advice on what makes a good social media policy. Your search, for example, social media policies should uncover one of my favorites is suggested by the **Mayo Clinic** (`http://network.socialmedia.mayoclinic.org/2012/04/05/a-twelve-word-social-media-policy/`):

Don't Lie, Don't Pry

Don't Cheat, Can't Delete

Don't Steal, Don't Reveal

Ready responses

Large companies can be a labyrinth of departments, managers, and experts, and it can be easy for employees to get lost, especially for HR advisors engaging with candidates through social media when there is no single point of responsibility for social media interactions. This is a challenge if one of your organization's risks is realized.

Let's consider an HR advisor who is responsible for maintaining the Facebook page for recruitment at an insurance firm: when a customer uses the recruitment page to complain about their insurance claim, how should they respond? What happens if it takes a couple of days to find the right person to provide an appropriate response? How about the HR advisor responsible for managing the Twitter feed from the careers team at a consultancy firm: when a candidate complains the recruitment process is unfair, what should their response be? What damage can be done if this isn't responded to quickly?

Creating some ready responses for your team empowers and equips them to respond in a timely and appropriate manner. Providing them with clearly identified referral points within the company gives them the support they can call upon when it's required.

Some key characteristics of good ready responses are as follows:

> **Consistent with the tone of the social media presence of the recruitment team:** If you aim to have a friendly and approachable tone, an overly legalistic response will strike a jarring note and impact on the relationships you are building

> **Empowering for team members working with social networking channels:** Your team needs to have your trust that they are authorized to represent the organization in providing a quick response, while providing them with clear boundaries for their authority

> **Approved by the appropriate authority:** Each response needs to be reviewed and approved by the department or manager who is responsible for handling the impact

A sample list of ready responses for an insurance company might look like this:

Trigger	Response	Further action	Approval
Customer complaint on the recruitment Facebook page	Your feedback is important to<brand name>; however, this page is aimed at our graduate recruitment community. I've forwarded your feedback to <enquiries e-mail address>.	Send details of comment to brand contact as described on HR wiki entry at <location to be advised>.	Marketing approver: to be advised (TBA) HR approver: TBA
Abusive or rude post on Twitter	No response.	Advise your leader for support if required.	Marketing approver: TBA HR approver: TBA

Trigger	Response	Further action	Approval
Defamatory or derogatory post on the recruitment Facebook page	Delete immediately with a comment "This post has been deleted because it violates our community guidelines. We encourage respectful conversation between all our community members."	Advise your leader for support if required.	Marketing approver: TBA HR approver: TBA
Questions regarding event such as flood or cyclone during active recruitment phase	This is a critical time for many of <brand name's> customers, please contact <recommended crisis contact point>.	Send details of comment to marketing contact as described on HR wiki entry at <location to be advised>.	Marketing approver: TBA HR approver: TBA Insurance brand approver: TBA
Complaint about recruitment process from a known candidate	We are sorry to hear about that. We will provide this important feedback to the team to review and improve their processes.	Call the candidate to sympathetically understand the details in private without committing to any action yet. Send details of comment to the HR advisor for assessment. Once assessed, provide a response to the candidate of the action being taken.	Marketing approver: TBA HR approver: TBA

Summary

There are serious landmines in your path as you navigate through the online world to execute a professional recruitment strategy. This is a new world with the rules of engagement still being written. This means that the HR department needs to be able to identify and understand the risks so that they can be mitigated and managed. The nature of social networks is one of immediacy and speed, so in order to manage risks in this world, your team needs to be able to act quickly and effectively. In this chapter we've worked through the steps to identify and understand the general risks of recruitment in an online world, as well as the unique and specific risks that apply to your industry and operating environment. This then forms the basis for a social media policy that provides guidance for all your employees on company expectations of their behavior while online and when representing the organization. We've also used this understanding of risks to create support for your team members representing your company online by providing them with ready responses to use if these risks are realized. In the next chapter, we'll build on this understanding of the risks to consider a plan that builds your team's capability as they develop their skills in using social networks as a channel for recruitment. Maintaining a keen awareness of the risks of this new world means that your organization is well placed to maximize the opportunities on offer.

3

Pulling it All Together in a Plan

"There is nothing new under the sun."

Although written thousands of years ago, this is a truism that applies to recruitment today. We're doing the same thing we did when we used to advertise in the local paper, invite someone we met at a social function to apply for a role, or hire someone who is a current employee's connection. The difference is that we're using modern platforms to reach potential candidates, and the advantage of these social platforms is that we can reach a niche audience more easily than ever before.

In this chapter, we'll build a staged approach to using social media channels as part of a recruitment strategy. We'll be using social networks to find and connect with potential hires in their own community with the aim to bring them into a community built around your employer brand. We'll also look at how four different organizations use social media platforms for recruitment.

There are two key parts to the strategy you're building: reaching a wide but targeted pool of potential candidates, and then building a relationship with the subset of candidates who are interested in working for your organization.

A staged approach

Now it's time to develop an implementation plan. The proposed plan is to take an iterative approach that builds confidence and capability as your team learns what works and what doesn't work, and continually refine and improve the effectiveness of their efforts.

Stage 1 – Preparing

The first stage is to prepare your social networking presence across multiple platforms and establish the structure and resources to engage through these platforms. This means taking stock of your presence. This may include the corporate careers page, your Facebook careers page, employee LinkedIn groups, and official careers Twitter accounts. Any gaps can be addressed by establishing a new presence consistent with your employer brand.

Your organizational structure will have a heavy influence on how you resource the work ahead. If your company has, or can establish, a dedicated social network team for HR, then this will provide the key resources to execute your plan. Alternatively, if you have identified the social mavens in your organization who can dedicate some of their time to supporting HR recruitment, you might choose to establish an "HR Socialites" virtual team of rotating employees who work with an HR advisor for a set amount of time, for example, 30 minutes each day.

Make a note

Case study 1: CH2M, an engineering and consulting company, established their careers landing page as their first step in establishing their presence, as can be seen at http://www.careers.ch2m.com/worldwide/en/europe.asp.

Stage 2 – Broadcasting

Just as when you started using Twitter, initially, the focus is on broadcasting information. Let's establish a starting point for Facebook and Twitter:

Facebook posts will be a mix of:

➤ Twice-weekly authoritative posts on interview techniques, career advice, and other updates from you HR department

➤ Weekly employee experience posts by current employees; these may include updates on their current role, or the latest initiatives they've worked on

➤ Weekly community engagement posts by different departments on their individual or team activities with community organizations

Twitter posts will be twice-daily, comprising:

➤ 60 percent of tweets with links to information across the Web

➤ 30 percent on job vacancies and corporate information

➤ 10 percent links to careers Facebook posts

To be honest, your starting point isn't the most important part. You can read any social media introduction and put in place a good enough approach based on generic guidelines. What really matters is to establish the metrics that will allow you to measure the impact of the approach and allow your team to adjust based on these measures. Your approach will be increasingly relevant to your organization, industry, and target audience for recruitment.

For example, you may choose to count the number of retweets and reposts as a measure of how popular particular types of posts are, and you might count the increase in new page followers after each post as a measure of their contribution to the growth of your community. You'll then do more or less of these particular posts based on the response from your community.

The content that you are building on your social networking platforms will continue to attract your target candidates to your employment brand and, over time, as you consistently contribute valuable content, your community will grow quickly.

Make a note

Case study 2: Deloitte Australia, a part of a global organization providing audit, consulting, financial advisory, risk management, and tax services, engage with the financial services community through broadcasting content from their Twitter account (*@FederalBudget*). You can find this at `http://www.deloitte.com/ assets/Dcom-Australia/Local%20Assets/Documents/Services/ Consulting/Deloitte_SocialNetworking_v6.pdf`.

Stage 3 – Conversing

Now that you're well practiced at engaging with others through Twitter, you can see the same principles at work through Facebook and LinkedIn discussion groups. This stage is the next logical step from the listening stage.

This is about building relationships with people who will form your community. It's an opportunity to forge a stronger relationship with candidates who may become employees, building a relationship between the candidate and the employer through responding and communicating to topics they are talking about.

As their interest grows, potential candidates start building a relationship with your employer brand.

It's worth encouraging your employees to maintain an active and relevant LinkedIn profile: many candidates will check the LinkedIn profile of their connections at your company as well as that of the hiring manager.

Make a note

Case study 3: Forrester, a global research and advisory firm, uses their Twitter account (`https://twitter.com/forresterjobs`) to connect with potential candidates, as they've found it is the fastest growing social networking channel in their recruitment strategy.

Stage 4 – Multichanneling

Just as you found different communities to connect to through your own journey to become a digital native, your identity as an employing organization should also grow while learning and increase its reach over time. At this stage, you should start to see the benefits of your multichannel approach as you combine traditional ways of connecting to potential candidates with the newer social network channels.

For example, your team may attend career fairs, and your stand at the career fair might include a Twitter hashtag for employees and candidates to tweet updates and questions; or you may suggest people visit your Facebook page to get a better idea of the work environment. You might also direct potential graduates to YouTube videos of graduates talking about their experience as new employees.

If you combine this approach with targeted metrics, you'll find your approach will change over time as you discover what has the most impact and where you want to invest your team's efforts.

Make a note

Case study 4: Sodexo, a management services company in the U.S., Canada, and Mexico, have established their employer brand's presence across multiple platforms such as their corporate careers page (`http://www.sodexo.com/en/careers/work-for-sodexo.aspx`), Facebook (`https://www.facebook.com/SodexoCareers`), YouTube (`http://www.youtube.com/user/SodexoCareers`), Twitter (`https://twitter.com/SodexoCareers`), and LinkedIn (`http://www.linkedin.com/groups?home=&gid=44261&trk=anet_ug_hm`).

Sourcing candidates

There are many varied approaches to sourcing candidates for vacant positions, and the success of each approach will depend on the ubiquitous or scarce population of candidates with the right skills and capabilities, the seniority of the roles, the geographic location of the employer, and many other factors. Let's consider some social-network-based approaches for sourcing candidates.

LinkedIn search

There is a lot of potential in LinkedIn's search capability for casting a wider net than just your careers community. The platform provides sophisticated search and tracking features that allows HR departments and recruiting firms to search through a large number of résumés that are held on this professional networking site. The search algorithms put an emphasis on people who fall within your own network, so the stronger your LinkedIn presence and the better your network is, the more effective is the search.

Employee networks

Ideally, you are able to tap into the wider workforce within your organization to expand your reach. Just imagine if two employees respond to a post about a job vacancy, and their response then reaches two hundred followers between them and, remembering that most of us connect with people in the same geographic area and in a similar age-group, then you've reached a wider audience of people who may not be actively looking for work, but could be a potential match.

One way to encourage your hiring managers and their team members to broadcast to their own network of friends and professional connections is to provide briefing notes that suggest a short post or tweet with a link to more information about the vacancy. This can be particularly effective when you remind your employees of any available rewards for referrals that lead to successful hires.

Advertising to people who are searching online

If you want to reach a wide audience, you might consider purchasing advertisements that will appear when people search for keywords. For example, when recruiting in a competitive IT talent market for data scientists, you could advertise to people searching for information on big data products such as Cassandra or Hadoop.

Summary

Through these chapters, you've built your personal skills and comfort level in navigating different social networks to find and connect with people and interests; these same skills you've then applied to build on your organization's recruitment strategy to find and connect with potential employees using social networks.

You've set up your team to build relationships between your employer and individuals in the wider online community: these relationships get closer as potential employees move through the stages from possible interest to being a candidate engaged in the recruitment process. Importantly, your team has the necessary support to confidently handle the possible issues, both general and unique to your industry, that can arise when using these new channels of communication for recruitment.

One of the advantages of a strategic approach is that, when done well, many of your employees become part of your recruitment team, as those employees with an influential social network presence understand and are able to support the company's strategy for using social networks for recruitment. What's key is taking an approach that is tailored to your company, and is continually being refined as the team learns and adapts.

By taking these steps, your organization can describe and see the purpose and value of social networking for HR managers and hiring leaders. As you execute against your recruitment strategy, you will realize the value of using social network channels to effectively and efficiently engage high-quality candidates and productive new employees.